Identity Crisis

THE ROOT OF IT'S BEGINNING

You Can Overcome

by
Carrie M. Carter

Copyright © 2015 by Carrie M. Carter

VMH Vikki M. Hankins™ Publishing
3355 Lenox Rd. NE Suite 750 Atlanta, GA 30326
www.vikkihankins.net

Without limiting the rights under copyright reserved above, no part of this publication may be reproduced, stored in or introduced into a retrieval system, or transmitted, in any form or by any means, without prior written permission of both the copyright owner and publisher of this book. Your support of the author's rights is appreciated.

Manufactured in the United States of America

Paperback ISBN: 978-0-9989653-9-0

Hardback ISBN: 978-0-9989653-8-3

10 9 8 7 6 5 4 3 2 1

Cover Design: Vikki Hankins
Cover Graphic: Shutterstock

Author's Note:
Some names and identifying details have been changed to protect the privacy of individuals. The events documented in this publication are according to the author's memory.

The publisher is not responsible for websites, or social media pages (or their content) that are not owned by the publisher. Further the publisher disclaims any liability to any party for any damage or disruption caused by errors or omissions by the author.

Contents

Dedication 5
Foreword 7
Introduction 9
Chapter 1   Beginning: the point of time or space
at which anything begins 13
Chapter 2   Identify: to associate in name, feeling,
interest, action 25
Chapter 3   Confront: to present for acknowledgment,
set face to face 39
Chapter 4   Conquer: to gain, win, overcome or
obtain by effort, to gain a victory 49
Chapter 5   Hope: indication of certainty, confident,
an expectation 59
Chapter 6   Deliverance: liberation, release, rescue,
emancipation 67
Chapter 7   Restoration: renewal, original, the act of
returning something that was stolen
or taken 77
Chapter 8   Walking In Victory! Victory: a success or
superior position achieved against an
opponent, opposition and difficulty 87

Dedication

With a grateful heart it is an honor and privilege to dedicate "Identity Crisis...the Roots of its Beginning" to my beloved dad, the late Larry D. Thompson.

Words cannot express the hero he was to my siblings & me. Larry D. Thompson, affectionately known as "Tee" took on a huge responsibility in providing paternal support to 4 children that were not his biological children. No one could ever tell him anything different concerning his relationship with us. He never allowed us to call him stepdad. The love he had for us was unconditional and real. It was through his love, guidance, correction and encouragement that I became who I am today. He would not allow us to settle concerning anything in life. With everything that he did, he put his heart fully into it. Although, we bumped heads for many years, it was through his dedication and steadfastness, that I begin to heal and stopped battling my own identity crisis. Through his life journey and awesome testimony I learned you can become and do whatever you set your heart and mind to do. He made up his mind early in life not to allow the pain from his past to hinder him from his own personal ambitions and aspirations. After being abandoned at the age of 3 months old in an abandoned home, he and his siblings were later adopted by a loving family that provided love and nurturing for which he subsequently provided to my sisters and me. He had his own experience with an "identity crisis" and feelings of rejection for which he allowed it to motivate him to do and be better. We were so proud of our dad and for his many accomplishments in life. He always echoed these words to us as life presented challenges, "to whom much is given much is required."

He wasn't perfect by far, but he was faithful to his family. He will forever be imbedded into our hearts. Thank you Deacon Larry D. Thompson for your love and for always seeing my potential and my destiny. You spoke life to me so many times and you saw the best in me. Thank you for remaining faithful when I didn't want you around, when the pain started to get real and was too much to bear. Thank you for not giving up on me! I love you forever, your "Lucky.

Lastly, I am committed to the cancer foundation you wanted to start and my efforts will be to bring it to fruition in your honor. The Larry D. Thompson Cancer Foundation, Fight of Hope! Through life obstacles you were always a fighter and you WON!

Foreword

It is estimated that more than seven billion people exist on planet earth, people from different cultures and different ethnicities. One thing that all of us on earth have in common is a need to answer what I call the questions of the human heart. Questions like, who am I, where am I from, what can I do, and where am I going. These Questions has all to do with identity, and if we do not get answers to these questions, we go through life frustrated and disappointed. Then Life becomes an experiment because we are not sure who we are and what our potential is. Pastor Carrie Carter, in her first printed book, and may I add many more to come, takes us on a journey to discover our true identity, she takes us back to the beginning of our origin to lay the foundation that will become our blueprint for life. With a mandate on her life to minister comfort, hope, deliverance, and restoration, to everyone that will take out the time to absorb the revelation of this book will be blessed. As her uncle I am very godly proud that she is willing to be transparent with her own identity crisis to help someone else Discover there's.

Dr. Norman Hutchins

Introduction

As I look around today at our nation as a whole, my heart is burdened and overwhelmed due to the number of hurting people.. Many are walking around as if there is no hope. I truly understand we're living in the 21st century in a world flooded with distresses like divorce, absent fathers, or mothers, rampant sexual abuse, terrorism, school shootings, bullying, highly increased domestic violence, suicide, gang violence, and so much more.

Due to the rapid increase of violence, financial struggles, and unemployment in homes at large, many are dwelling in depression, oppression, or have just suppressed their pain, by either medicating or masking it. I often ponder questions to myself, "How did we get here and where did it begin?" The purpose of my writings is to convey the beginning of how something so delicate can end up being so deadly. I am a firm believer everything begins with a seed in order for it to grow or manifest. There is power in one seed so as it is in the natural, it is in the spiritual. If you plant one seed, water it and cultivate it, the fruit from the seed doesn't grow immediately but over time you will eventually reap a harvest of its fruit if not uprooted before its time. Therefore, in our lives one negative or positive seed can be planted and can change the course of our path. Growing up, we use to have a saying, "Sticks and stones may break my bones but words can never hurt.". As I got older I understood more that it's a myth. Words "hurt" and take "root".

It's my desire that everyone that would ever read this book "Identity Crisis, the Root and It's Beginning" will understand that a seed was planted during our adolescent stages. The things I mentioned in the introduction aren't things that just happened, but it's a battle of the mind and many are still battling identity. Beginning in adolescence, many of us failed to achieve identity during that period for whatever reason, which in the interim caused us to face physical growth, integrate ideas of ourselves, as well as what others thought of us. It also formed a self-image resolving in crisis. This sort of unresolved crisis leaves us struggling to find ourselves, seeking negative identity, which involved crimes, drugs, love in all the wrong places or the inability to make defining choices about the future and will eventually lead to a victim mentality.

As you take this journey with me while reading this book, you will understand why I used the word

Identity Crisis: the Root of Its Beginning

"us"! I too suffered an identity crisis from youth to adulthood. My goal is to restore hope and understanding that all things are possible, especially if the wound is deep. I am a living testimony that no matter how deep the wound may be, healing and wholeness can be your portion. We were created and destined for purpose, while the plan of enemy is to steal, kill and destroy. Surely we can attest to that as we turn on the news every day.

There is a "root" cause to many good or bad decisions. If a tree is planted, and it is cut down, the "root" is still there. In other words, many have planted bad or good seeds and we often harbor the bad seeds, keeping them hostage in our subconscious mind, and allowing them to grow up with us and in us. Through this book, we are going to slay every giant that has lain dormant for years. The Word of God declares "He sent his word, and healed them, and delivered them from their destructions." (Ps. 107:20) Identity crisis will eventually lead to destruction if not confronted and combated. As you begin to read, please have pen and paper to journal your hurts, pains, fears, rejection, etc. I have already sought God on your behalf and we are going to uproot the pain of the past to walk in our true identity. We are unique in our own way, every man, woman, boy and girl. The ultimate goal is that you be encouraged, built-up and whole in every facet of your life! That can only be done by identifying the pain, confronting the hurt, and conquering what has conquered the mind, walking in total victory knowing God's Word alone is effective to heal, restore hope, and deliver.

Chapter 1

Beginning: the point of time or space at which anything begins

First, we must understand that everything that exists started with a beginning. "In the beginning God created the heavens and earth. And the earth was without form, and void; and darkness was upon the face of the deep...." (Gen. 1:1-2) Everything that was, was spoken into existence. In the beginning the earth was void; there was nothing. God Himself spoke everything into existence that would ever live. It didn't just happen overnight, but it was done in a course of six days. On the final day, the sixth day God created man. "So God created man in his own image, the image of God created he him; male and female created he them"(Gen 1:27). We are reflections of God's Glory, imitators of Christ. We will never be totally like God for He is our supreme Creator. But we do have the ability to reflect his character in our love, patience, forgiveness, kindness and faithfulness.

But Eve was deceived. "For God doth know that in that day ye eat thereof, then your eyes shall be opened, you will become just like God"(Gen 3:5). In the beginning, we were already created in the image of God; Satan used a sincere motive to tempt Eve for it wasn't wrong of Eve to want to be like God. To become more like God is humanity's highest goal. What took place is that deception and an identity crisis came into play. Eve, unknowing of her own identity, was founded in Christ, at the very beginning. She was then deceived in hopes to be just like God, yet defying God's authority, thus trying to take God's place. This was primarily due to deception, the state of being deceived; a fraud. Crisis fell upon both Adam and Eve; it was an emotionally significant event or radical change of status in a person's life resulting in spiritual death being their portion. As we examine how Satan deceived Eve, let us be mindful that he uses many of these same devices and tactics with us today. He speaks to us in our thoughts, through other people, through situations, through our flesh and emotions. He uses temptations, and ambitions of wanting to get ahead, and to prosper, by getting more things, with the hopes of thinking that more things will make us happy or feel important, but never understanding the basis of who we are or why we were created.

Many walk around feeling so hopeless, lifeless and despondent to life. Identity crisis is more widespread than most people are aware. We all have the propensity for an identity crisis. As stated in the introduction, it's an adolescent problem and its foundation occurs as many are growing into manhood or womanhood. It has caused many to be stagnated in life, not understanding what was causing this condition. It can stem from the smallest thing, i.e. me getting upset as a child because my mom brought my sister a better looking doll than the one I had. Sounds really childish, right? But as small as its sounds, it begins a sense of identity crisis and it begins to increase with age and through stages in life. Many alter their appearance to look identical to someone else, due to not liking who they are. Superiority complex among colleagues, unhealthy competition, and brown nosing all scream a sense of identity crisis. Are you unsure of who you are? Do you spend the majority of your time pleasing others and wanting to be just like someone else? Do you fish for compliments and accolades? Please know admiring a person or being greatly influence or inspired by someone is totally different and is a very good thing. But are you asking yourself why you are not this or that? If so, you may be experiencing identity crisis. Identity crisis can be a deadly thing and it robs us from life and walking life out in an authentic way.

In research and understanding the nature of identity, it's a collection of an individual's thoughts, desires, memories consciousness and beliefs. In others words, many feel the body directly alters the personality of an individual, but does not understand the body contains the identity of an individual. Identity Crisis is found when a person is struggling to find their identity. Not one person was born with the same identity; we will never contain the same fingerprints and this holds true for identical twins, even though they're identical. Every human being is a unique individual, with our own personality, likes, dislikes, thoughts and feelings. Identical twins are no different; they may look the same but they are not the same person and it is not fair to treat them as such. Life has dealt some hard blows, while expecting everyone to operate with the same understanding. We also must accept the challenge of embracing one's differences and uniqueness while learning to be ourselves. I mentioned earlier that identity crisis can be deadly; it also can cause rejection, bitterness, and resentment, sometimes to the ones closest to you.

And in the process of time it came to pass that Cain brought an offering of the fruit of the ground to the lord. Abel also brought of the firstborn of his flock and their fat. And the Lord respected Abel and his offering, but He did not respect Cain and his offering. And Cain was very angry, and his countenance fell. So the Lord said to Cain, Why are you angry? And why has your countenance fallen? Now Cain talked with Abel his brother; and it came to pass, when they were in the field, that Cain rose up against Abel his brother and killed him (Gen 4:3-8).

Like Cain we can be victims of an identity crisis that leads to death, if not mastered or dealt with in its early stages. Are you fighting for something that wasn't accomplished in your earlier years? Or screaming for attention that was never given? Is there a void in your heart that is causing painful insecurities? Do you find yourself being arrogant? These things are just causing us not to perform to our highest ability due to not dealing with it. Yet instead we become a victim to the root of its beginning. Jacob then lied and tricked his father into believing he was Esau so Isaac blessed him. Esau sold his birthright to his brother Jacob for a bowl of lentil stew. Identity crisis came into action with the two brothers as bitterness was developed between the two and turned into a plan to murder his own brother. As I stated, it is so easy to happen when we don't know our own worth and value. Many become eager to get ahead instead of growing in the process. Jacob found himself for many years running and continuing with the same character because it was deeply rooted. It became a part of his everyday life for Jacob was known as a trickster and deceiver as he battled identity issues.

I've worked with the Criminal Justice system well over 19 years; over 35 % of our caseloads deal with obtaining property by false pretense and identity theft, where many are trying to get ahead using someone else's identity. The enemy comes to steal, kill and destroy. Steal our identity, kill our purpose and ultimately destroy our destiny! Please understand, we do have choices, by no means should this behavior be accepted or permitted. When a behavior has been rooted in your heart since birth, it becomes a part of your life until you identify its root and uproot it from the core. So, Jacob knew he couldn't flee from his brother for the rest of his life, running over twenty years. That's a long time right? That's just how serious identity crisis is, and how long it can go undetected and exist in a person. However, I have good news that "you can overcome!" Jacob finally had to go back to his hometown which meant he had to face his brother head on. He spent the night in agony. Have you ever been there? Have you ever been in a place where you were tired of the agony and relentless pain? This caused Jacob to have a personal encounter with God himself; he wrestled with God all night, and demanded he wouldn't let go until God blessed him. Many would suggest a material blessing, but how many know you can have all the material blessings in the world, but have no peace or joy. Jacob said, "Even though I met with God face to face, I am still alive."

Identity Crisis: the Root of Its Beginning

Jacob's name and his character were changed due to one encounter with God and his brother Esau was able to forgive him. Unforgiveness has crippled so many of us. There is nothing too hard for God no matter how long you have wrestled with yourself and circumstances. You can overcome identity crisis no matter how deep the root may be. We cannot do it in our own strength or ability. Let's OVERCOME together! I've worked with the Criminal Justice system well over 19 years; over 35 % of our caseloads deal with obtaining property by false pretense and identity theft, where many are trying to get ahead using someone else's identity. The enemy comes to steal, kill and destroy. Steal our identity, kill our purpose and ultimately destroy our destiny! Please understand, we do have choices, by no means should this behavior be accepted or permitted. When a behavior has been rooted in your heart since birth, it becomes a part of your life until you identify its root and uproot it from the core. So, Jacob knew he couldn't flee from his brother for the rest of his life, running over twenty years. That's a long time right? That's just how serious identity crisis is, and how long it can go undetected and exist in a person. However, I have good news that "you can overcome!" Jacob finally had to go back to his hometown which meant he had to face his brother head on. He spent the night in agony. Have you ever been there? Have you ever been in a place where you were tired of the agony and relentless pain? This caused Jacob to have a personal encounter with God himself; he wrestled with God all night, and demanded he wouldn't let go until God blessed him. Many would suggest a material blessing, but how many know you can have all the material blessings in the world, but have no peace or joy. Jacob said, "Even though I met with God face to face, I am still alive." Jacob's name and his character were changed due to one encounter with God and his brother Esau was able to forgive him. Unforgiveness has crippled so many of us. There is nothing too hard for God no matter how long you have wrestled with yourself and circumstances. You can overcome identity crisis no matter how deep the root may be. We cannot do it in our own strength or ability. Let's OVERCOME together!

Your Thoughts

Your Thoughts

Your Thoughts

Your Thoughts

Chapter 2

Identify: to associate in name, feeling, interest, action

Many may know me as a very sweet loving and caring person, that always smiles and would go the distance for anyone, especially the underdog, but not many knew me as the bitter, fearful, angry, rejected little girl that battled identity crisis through adulthood. Allowing bitterness to linger for a period of time led to resentment, which caused me to be easily offended. I harbored many disappointments that germinated in my heart. As a child I could not pin point my bitterness. It wasn't until I got into my adolescent stages that I began to identify my issues. Growing up, I will never forget when asked why they called me "Lucky" which is my nickname; I was always ashamed to answer. Even though my mom was pregnant with me, she decided to party all night at the night club because she loved to dance. Well, on this particular night, I guess I decided to enter into the world early. We all lived with my grandmother in those days and there was no such thing as central air conditioning and heating. We had pot belly stoves to use to stay warm. So again, on this particular night I decided to come forth before my actual due date. My mom was walking in my grandmother's kitchen and I literally came out so quickly that I almost dropped into the pot belly stove. My grandmother caught me before I hit the fire so from that point on, I was called "Lucky." Even after that, according to my mom and grandmother, at the age of four, they recalled me hollering and screaming for my mom. It was because my oldest sister had me on the bed, flat on my back jumping up and down on my stomach wanting me dead. I lived through that and then at the age of five, she tried to drown me.

I couldn't understand why my own sister wanted me dead. It wasn't until I found out she did not want any siblings and she wanted to be an only child. I in turn grew up bitter asking myself a question, "Why are you still living…you are not loved." I am the second to the oldest child. I have two younger siblings among my mother's children. I always admired my siblings, especially my oldest sister and the youngest girl. I remember my oldest sister spending a lot of time with her biological father as we grew up in the same household. I didn't realize then how blessed we were to have a very special step dad in our lives that truly cared. He never allowed us to call him "step dad" nor did he call us his step children. He would always say these are my children. He accepted us all as his own biological children. As a child, I always wanted to follow my oldest sister. I loved how she would always say "her dad" in reference to her biological father. Growing up I understood more and more why I loved to hear it; it was something I deeply craved and desired. I always wanted to be daddy's little girl, although we had our "step dad" in our lives. There was a void in my heart that triggered some deep issues in life. As a child, I didn't know who my biological father was. Although our mother loved us so dearly and did her best raising and caring for us, there was certainly a void due to the absence of my biological father. I couldn't grasp or understand why a father would be absent in their child's life. The thought of this impacted me and started what many would call "feeling rejected" and bitterness began to set in even more. I began to act out my hurt in my behavior and I became disrespectful to our stepfather. Hindsight being 20/20, I now understand that it was not done intentionally, but out of anger and from a broken place.

In addition to my biological father not being in my life, I felt insecure about my siblings being extremely smart while I struggled through school. In my household, I was known as the least likely to succeed. The complexity of my own identity manifested fully during this time. The crisis became evident in my school years and this is when a victim's mentality developed and it became my place of escape. I started dating all the wrong guys and many were much older than me. I did this in hopes of feeling better about myself. Deep down I just wanted to feel love and acceptance. As the void grew deeper, I began asking myself over and over again, "What is wrong with me?" Inevitably my mind would play games on me especially while dealing with pain after pain and hurt after hurt. I could hear in my own mind "nobody cares about you", "you are not smart," you are not pretty," and "your father abandoned you." There was a war in my mind and the sad thing is that I believed all of the lies in my hearing. I started wishing to be someone else, anyone else. It was no longer a place of admiring a person or my siblings but I wanted to be them. I can recall in my mind saying, "Oh I wish I had their beauty, hair, shape, smartness, etc." I never wanted to take my own life, but there were many days that I could care less if the sun didn't shine or if I didn't live to see the next day. I just didn't care if I wasn't happy with who I was. When dating guys, I could never understand what they really saw in someone like me. Then again, was it all about them? I was honestly looking for love in all the wrong places.

Identity Crisis: the Root of Its Beginning

I will never forget my step dad kicking me out of the house because I became defiant by staying out late at night. This one particular night when I came home, I returned to find all of my belongings boxed up and on the front porch. Wow, that shocked me in a great way. I can laugh about it now but then I was furious. For me it was hurtful for a parent to do anything like this. In my mind, I could not understand how my stepfather would kick me out of my mother's house or how she would allow him to do so. My defense was he wasn't my real father. What I didn't fully understand was that he was my mother's husband; he paid the bills and he was creating boundaries for our home.

I was left in search of myself as I was making a lot of bad decisions. I once again ended up in the arms of the wrong guy and he wanted more than I could give. I was getting ready to leave his home one day and he demanded that I stay. In the middle of our conversation, he left the room and came back with a gun in his hand. He pointed it directly in my face. My whole life flashed before my eyes and I felt numbed with no ability to move out of fear for my life. All I could do was cry inside and outside while asking him the question, "Why?" I didn't understand prayer then like I know now. It is the effectual fervent prayer of the righteous that avails much! However, I knew there were stored up prayers that my grandmother prayed for me. As I cried out, begging and pleading for my life and for him to let me go, he would not. A few minutes later, I heard a door open and later discovered that it was his sister coming home from school early because she was sick. She didn't know what was going on in the other room, but thank God for orchestrating her return home. That day, she was my guardian angel. It was then that I realized I had to grab a hold of life and get myself on track. It was as if my life was doing a downward spiral and my end didn't look good at all based on the course I was on.

My reality check was while I wanted to be like everyone else, a major crisis was taking place in me. This was a great opportunity for me to get on the road to discovering myself, my self-worth and the value that I brought to life. It came apparent to me that happiness is a choice and we cannot depend on circumstances to dictate our happiness or who we are as individuals. Identifying the issues that lie within is the biggest step one can take. All that we are willing to reveal and release will make room for healing to take place. First, identify the problem and then diagnosis the reasons for our worries, anxiety, tension, bitterness, resentment, fears, and anger. Trust me in saying that all of these characteristics come from somewhere. If the underlying pain or issue is never dealt with but is constantly being swept under the rug, it will only create more clutter and make things worse. Many things over the course of life has been planted and taken root within us. They remain dormant in the subconscious mind over time. The subconscious mind can hold a memory bank as early as the age of five (5) years old. But another uninvited guest could show up and he is called hypertension or stress, which is a silent killer. Both can very easily lead to depression and/or a mental illness. The first thing a person does when he or she attends Alcoholic Anonymous is admit that they have a problem. If there is no admittance to the issue, there will be no resolution to this issue. I have said all of this to say, I had to first admit to identifying that I was hurt and acknowledged the pain I felt. When we visit the doctor for an appointment and the doctor asks where it hurt, we are quick to explain every pain, ache and discomfort to the doctor because we want relief. All we know is that we are hurting and want a diagnosis or solution in order to feel and be better, In the same manner, when anger, bitterness and rage rare up, it's time to identify by seeking help and sharing our wounds. It was a must that I began my quest to better understand what was going on inside of me. It was essential for me to identify the root of my issues. I later discovered that it all stemmed back to the rejection, not feeling loved and not knowing my own identity or self-worth. The absence of my father and the fact that he didn't take the initiative to build a relationship with me deeply disturbed me. I spent my childhood, college years and some of my adulthood looking for acceptance and validation. Circumstances in my life caused me to evaluate myself and began to identify with my hurt and dissatisfaction. I was making a lot of bad decisions and found myself in some of the most peculiar situations. There was a scar on my heart that needed to be healed. As with every scar there is a process to it being healed. . I had to take my journey for healing and process of discovery step by step until I was able to see past the fear, shame and discontentment. There were some areas I really thought I had already been healed in until I saw that to be touched in that area brought about tears in my eyes and pain in my heart.

The Word of God declares, "Where no counsel is, the people fall; but in the multitude of counselors there is safety" (Proverbs 11:14). After identifying the areas of pain, the next step for me was safety. This was the point in my life that brought about change and a major transformation. Our identity is found in Christ Himself, but if not identified early, we carry low self-esteem and insecurities into adulthood. I have often heard people say "Time heals all wounds" but what I discovered is that sometimes, time make wounds worse. When we allow behaviors and issues to go unattended, we give them free course to take root and build up residue. I am convinced that God in time heals all wounds as we yield ourselves to the process of becoming better and whole. There comes a time when you just have to deal with issues head on by the grace of God and applying the Word of God. It doesn't always come easy because confronting one's self is no easy task because it feels like you have to walk through agony all over again. However, it is needful as it helps us in the long run and gives us victory over the things that once controlled and manipulated us. No matter how many bumps and bruises you encounter in life, you're still important to God. The Word of God says "For you died, and your life is hidden with Christ in God, it's a matter of us dying to our nature (identity) and accepting the nature of Christ, our identity is found in him. I will praise you, for I am fearfully and wonderfully made; marvelous are your works" (Col. 3:3; Ps. 139:14). Have you ever gone to the grocery store to purchase canned goods? While looking for your favorite brand, or brand of choice, you see several cans that are banged up, bruised, or where the outside is crushed. We tend to overlook those disfigured cans because their packaging is unappealing. We either overlook them or put them towards the back of the shelf. In other words, we have been so damaged, mistreated, dropped, thrown to the back of line, we wonder will it ever be our turn. Many of us have suffered just as that can did, but we don't always realize right away that the content is still good and is the same as the cans that are sitting nicely on the shelf. Often times we over look our value and worth due to looking through foggy lenses. We must know and understand that we are fearfully and wonderfully made. Despite the hardship and unfairness in life, marvelous (superb, excellent, astonishment, extraordinary) are thy works. When God created us He produced jewels in His own image. Might I submit to every reader to identify the place of it's (the issue or crisis) beginning and write it on paper. List the areas of pain if you can, see what the word of God says about it and take the necessary steps of prayer and accountability to address them. Once this is done, you are now free from at least 90% of your issues by simply identifying them. I know firsthand, if not identified, confronted and conquered it will plague your life, marriage, career and even your parenting ability!

Your Thoughts

Your Thoughts

Your Thoughts

Your Thoughts

Chapter 3

Confront: to present for acknowledgment, set face to face

After we are able to identify the issues (seed embedded), time will come to address the root of the issue, which are the real problems and generally the actual sources of the underlining concerns. Do know in doing this, there will be issues for which we are too afraid to address head on, but confronting them is a must in order to combat what is combating us. How do we confront it? We must deal with it, by not running from it, or being a flight risk or shifting blame, as well as not saying my life would have been so much better if he or she would have been a part of it. Whether we take action and confront to forgive or confront ourselves, we can choose to deal with it head on in love. A soft answer turns away wrath. At times identifying the issue is difficult because in essence, it becomes a part of your reality yet no longer a place of comfort. Confronting it can be a battle within itself, but it is so vitally important.

There will be times when we will pour out of our heart as we confront a person, or situation. It is likely that the other person may never have an explanation as to why they hurt us and they may not even assume any responsibility for it. What I have come to realize is that hurt people hurt people and healed people heal people. Sometimes we cannot fault people because of where they are mentally, emotionally or physically. However, we are all accountable for our actions. Often times we do things that impact others negatively, unaware of our actions and its great effects. With this, there are times where it is a matter of choice to let go and allow God to work in the situation. Eventually with life and as we mature, wisdom will teach us how to move forward, especially after you have exhausted yourself. We have to know we were chosen before the foundation of the world to carry no one else's identity, but our own. We often think climbing the corporate ladder of success or receiving another rank in Christendom identifies the authentic you. By no means is success or elevation a bad thing! But it is just imperative that we aren't masking who we are through success and still battling an identity crisis within ourselves. At no time should we attempt to cover it up with accolades or try to make up for someone we were not or something we did not achieve while growing up, as well as moving from place to place in a seemingly endless quest to find happiness. Even when moving or relocating to new surroundings, we are still carry the same person from the previous location and still facing the same struggles and challenges. If confrontation is avoided, there will always be a war within; peace we will never come into touch with our true feelings to know there is sadness and pain buried inside and no amount of success will ever make us happy. It will keep requiring more pressure to becoming even greater, but with a wounded heart, an identity crisis will continue to rob us from the flow of life.

Habitually we identity ourselves with what we have accomplished or what others have deemed us to be, rarely do we identity the loving, caring, beautiful/handsome person that is within. Beauty is skin deep, not surface deep. You can encounter the most attractive person in the world but if he or she is insecure in who they are, then in return he or she can be a very unpleasant or unattractive person due to masked pain. "But the Lord said to Samuel, Don't judge by his appearance or height, for I rejected him. The Lord doesn't see things the way you see them. People judge by outward appearance, but the Lord looks at the heart." (1 Sam 16:7) We tell ourselves it is safe to stay in a protected place and to guard our hearts and never confront anything. King David confronted a nine- foot giant at an early age, which prepared him for life. How do we confront our giant?

Identifying them is the first step. Honor our feelings and don't feel bad for getting in touch with your feelings. Growing up we were often told by our parents and many of you may know the saying as well, "What happens in our house stays in our house!" I truly appreciate my parents for the wisdom, but on another note, many of the dark secrets that are being confined to the secrets of one's house hurts more than allowing them to be released. Confront them and don't run; the more attempts to run away from reality, eventually has reality following us. We will never conquer what we aren't willing to confront. After maturing and finally embracing how to deal with confrontation or a confronting situation, I was more likely to try and be the peace maker when it came to difficult problems. I did this in hope of being accepted due to the identity crisis I once battled. In order to confront the problem, we cannot avoid the underlining issue, not the issue on the surface. Usually we tend to get upset with the surface issue, but actually it's much deeper, especially if we go from 1 to 10 in a second. Please don't avoid the issue; confront the reality face to face. The longer I avoided the pain of hurt and disappointments, the more enslaved I became to the pain. I will never forget a very devastating moment in life that I had no control over; hearing someone I love so deeply getting raped by multiple guys while being locked up in the next room. For many years, I avoided the incident as if it never happened in hopes to block out the realty of it. Life became a compounded situation for me and I then realize if I didn't confront this battle, especially after identify it, that it would continue to follow me. I remember one year after returning from a trip, I was talking with a really dear friend that I could just really be transparent with and I began to share past hurts and failures, as well as those I hurt along the way due to my hurt and even some that I hurt out of ignorance. That was a night of release; it was from that point that I knew I could no longer hold my biological father hostage for not been in the early stages of my life. I learned some of my behaviors were just excuses to make excuses and not to excel and there were some that were valid hurt that I needed to be healed and delivered from. My identity crisis came from self-inflicted wounds that I would never shed light to while keeping everything in a dark room with a false hope of one day being delivered. YOU cannot conquer reality by running away from it!

Your Thoughts

Your Thoughts

Your Thoughts

Your Thoughts

Your Thoughts

Chapter 4

Conquer: to gain, win, overcome or obtain by effort, to gain a victory

We will never be able to conquer our issues or walk into our true identity if we never identify and confront them. Courage is believed to be the most important quality in a man.Courage is the first of human virtues because it makes all of the others possible. The Lord spoke to Joshua and commanded him to be strong and of good courage. This quality was necessary for Joshua to take on the task at hand. The Lord reminded Joshua, as I was with Moses I will be you; if not careful once we have identified and confronted many deep rooted issues, the pressure of others could very well cause us to convert back to our identity crisis. Joshua could never be Moses, but God promised to be with him. I am sure like Joshua in our journey of life; we have felt inadequate and incapable before we even fought the first battle. God's plan is for us to conquer every giant as I mentioned in the previous chapter. King David confronted a nine foot giant. By confronting his giant, he also conquered him. We must conquer every physical, financial, emotional, family, employment and academic giant that has caused us to live in crisis mode. We have to change our language as well as our perception of how it's viewed. Had King David constantly complained about the magnitude of his gigantic giant, the giant would have continued to grow even larger in his view. Instead of King David listening to the voice of reasoning and of why he wasn't able to slay the giant, despite age, or height or his body build, I'm inclined to believe he chose to listen to the inward voice that said, "I can do all things through Christ which strengtheneth me" (Phil. 4:13). His life was already predestined to conquer [win] and his strength was made perfect in God. King David conquered one of the greatest battles, once he took on his biggest problems. It was then that the smaller problems took flight. In other words, once we identify and confront, we conquer every battle big or small. Just know every battle will not be the same nor have the same outcome, but don't be afraid tackle it head on in wisdom. All things work together for the good which includes the good, bad, ugly and indifferent. God cannot heal what we are not willing to reveal.

Although it may seem as if we are losing, learn to celebrate every victory big or small. I am a huge advocate for having your moment; it is okay to feel what you feel since it is vitally important to not quit in the moment. After you have had your moment, hold your head up, square your shoulders back and stay the course! Once I came in touch with my feelings, uprooting years of pain and the real issue of my identity crisis which also led me to feeling rejected, I finally had to conquer my giant of always wanting to be "daddy's little girl." After many tears and wise counsel, I finally understood that it wasn't my fault or anything that I did. At that time I didn't realize that my biological father had to work through hardships of his own and just maybe if he would have been in the early stages of my life, what impact would it really have had? Would I be where I am in life at this very moment? Or would my life have been worse off? I said that to say this, as hard as it is to digest, there is a reason why many have experienced the absence of their mother/father growing up or even their whole life. It's certainly difficult and often times it brings on so many mixed feelings, emotions and a sense of abandonment. On this quest, I've learned we can be healed step by step by identifying the pain and not allowing that place to hold us hostage. We have to refuse to remain the victim who leads us to a victim mentality, eventually becoming stagnated and causing us to make excuses to not excel or achieve greater things in life. We were created for a purpose, whether our entrance into this world was planned or unplanned by our parents. If it was a surprise or even an accident, the fact of the matter is that we were already on the mind of God. "Before I formed you in the womb I knew you, before you were born I set you apart; I appointed you a prophet to the nations" (Jeremiah 1:5). Jeremiah was on the mind of God and his purpose was already established. We can't afford to allow our circumstances, past or present situations to dictate our purpose. Purpose sought us out first before we encountered any disappointments. It is imperative that we now learn to veto, evict and uproot every negative seed that we have allowed to take up residence or root in our heart and mind. God has planned and prepared paths just for us. He has prearranged, orchestrated our unique purpose without being cloned to anyone else's purpose. Purpose will call you out, it will beckon you. Our purpose will motivate, drive and give a sense of hope, expectancy of our future. Our purpose will call us to the deeper things in God to awaken truth. Facts are misleading but the truth always prevails. In other words, facts depicted my battle with my own identity, all of my disappointments, all kinds of emotional setbacks but the truth prevailed in spite of life and its obstacles. I was still created for PURPOSE! The truth is there will be struggles, hardship as well as ongoing disappointments but we don't have to be or remain a hostage to it. We don't know God's plan for our lives, but we must trust His will and character.

Although, my biological father wasn't in the early stages of my life, I am so thankful God allowed him to be a part of the plan for my life. He had his own giants to fight by confronting them with courage. This allowed him to conquer them and live. Even now with tears streaming down my face, I write not with tears of pain any longer, but tears of joy with gratefulness for my daddy (Earnest Cox) whom I love dearly. "Courage is the most important of all the virtues, because without courage you can't practice any other virtue consistently. You can practice any virtue erratically, but nothing consistently without courage." - Maya Angelou

True personal growth only happens when we move forward, and that only happens when we have strength and courage to face every giant! True courage is risking comfort in order to conquer. The greatest battle we face is often the battle within ourselves, but the most fulfilling battle is when it's CONQUERED!

Your Thoughts

Your Thoughts

Your Thoughts

Your Thoughts

Your Thoughts

Chapter 5

Hope: indication of certainty, confident, an expectation

Every situation is very well a real situation, but, it doesn't have to remain a hopeless one! There is a saying that I often quote, pretty much every day and my church family knows it well. They are probably quoting it with me now... "Life happens and it happens to us all." We can either grow bitter or better from life but whatever you do remain hopeful. "Let us hold fast the profession of our faith without wavering; for he is faithful that promised" (Hebrews 10:23). When we experience the dark season of life and feel despair as if we are walking around wandering aimlessly due to the cares of life, we have to hold on to our faith yet believing He is faithful that promised.

Hope can be restored despite any situation. Abraham's hope wasn't in his own ability to father a child. It was rooted in faith trusting God. It is easy to place our hope in what we can see, taste, touch or feel. These things are natural and things we can control. Hope is at its best when you have to hope against hope for something that hasn't happened yet. I do my best to be confident while walking in expectation, sometimes with tears streaming down my face, not knowing God's next move but just trusting His timing. In the waiting process is where our hope is tried. The process of life is inevitable. The bible declares, "Hope deferred makes the heart sick: but when the desire cometh, it is a tree of life" (Proverbs 13:12). Hope displaced seems to make us remain on a never ending roller coaster ride from hopeful to hopelessness. This alone causes many to become angry with God as well as with others, especially seeing others being blessed and our blessings remaining so out of reach often times. It's easier to be full of hope and excitement when it looks like our desires will be fulfilled, and then emotionally drained on the account of "deferred hope" which means to "delay" or "draw out." That implies it is only delayed not denied, although it feels that way. This is when we have to hope against hope. We must endure the process by remaining hopeful even when the promise remains unseen. "Now faith is the substance of things hoped for, the evidence of things not seen" (Hebrew 11:1). Again, facts are misleading, but the truth always prevails! Even though it's my reality, it's not my actuality. Real faith is when God Who can do it chooses not to and you serve Him anyway.

Just know if God said it, it has to happen. We don't know God's ways or His plan. We only know what He has revealed through the Holy Spirit, so we must trust His character and his track record of never failing us, nor leaving or forsaking us. "Cast not away therefore your confidence, which hath great recompense of reward" (Hebrew 10:35).

As I encourage myself, it's also an honor to encourage everyone else. It's my prayer that someone is being encouraged right now as they read this book. Cast not away your confidence (trust, hope, expectation) but remain faithful. It is a crucial hour for movement and progression. We have come too far to draw back, despite the struggles and setbacks of life. Tough times don't last always. God promised to never leave or forsake us. We have an anchor in Jesus Christ our Lord. So just know it may be "deferred" at this present moment but when the desire cometh, it will be a tree of life, a time of refreshing. In other words, hearts will be relieved from the heaviness of the wait and delay by receiving the blessing and fruit of our labor.

Your Thoughts

Your Thoughts

Your Thoughts

Your Thoughts

Your Thoughts

Chapter 6

Deliverance: liberation, release, rescue, emancipation

It's often said or quoted" once an alcoholic you're always an alcoholic once you're an addict you're always an addict." Well I beg to differ; our actions or bad decisions do not have to remain our identity. We all needed deliverance from something at some time in our lives and may be battling something at this very moment, whether it is drugs, alcohol, sexual immorality, depression, fear, worry, or bondage. But whatever the case may be, we can be free! I am reminded of the parable of the prodigal son who wanted his worthy portion early. And when he received it, he wasted his possessions in reckless living. Once he spent everything and was left with nothing, hitting rock bottom, the Scripture tells us that he found himself in a place that he never imagined until he finally came to himself. In other words, there are times our deliverance or release will not come until we come to ourselves allowing pride to be a nonfactor. The biggest trick of the enemy is deception to deceive, distract, and camouflage our situation in hopes to make God seem distant and make us think that we will never be liberated from the pain of life and that it will always be that way. But not so! There is a joy, peace and happiness in being free. It wasn't until I got older that I realized this truth. I came to myself and stopped holding on to pain or blaming others for my bad choices. Yes, it's easier to hold on to pain than to release it. And yes, it's so much easier to continue to hold others hostage while making excuses not to deal with our insecurities, fears, or rejection. Although painful events happened in our lives, it's our responsibility to maintain our freedom. Freedom is quite costly, as well as the battle to get free and the battle to remain free. God gave Adam freedom of choice saying, "Of every tree of the garden, thou mayest freely eat, but of the tree of the knowledge of good and evil, thou shalt not eat of it:" (Genesis 2:16-17a). This stills holds true for us today; we have a choice to remain in bondage or walk in freedom. There are times we are delivered from some trials instantly while other deliverances are a process, especially if it is a stronghold that we have wrestled with for many years. Although we haven't been freed from it as of yet, it doesn't mean we cannot be free. So never get discouraged, but keep pressing for freedom, which is so vitally important.

Often times we shift different addictions i.e. we may not drink, but will shop all day to not confront pain, or eat excessively to deal with stress. The goal or objective of deliverance is wholeness; being healed and whole is crucial. I married my college sweetheart Jaycee in whom, I am so thankful for, but I now know that being whole in your singleness or working towards deliverance before marriage is very important. Speaking from a real place, I wasn't whole or healed before getting married in my early twenties and I carried my identity crisis into our marriage which caused a fence around my heart due to hidden wounds and unforgiveness. Although I loved my husband very much, I truly didn't know how to love on the level of being a wife at that time. If not careful we can allow the really good men/women to pay for something that the wrong man/woman did to us or find ourselves seeking a mother/father in our spouses, due to a void of an absent parent. It wasn't until I pursued an intimate relationship with God, pulling down the strongholds and patterns of life that had me in bondage and seeking my inner healing. Truly I learned how to love myself first and foremost, so I could love with a pure heart. I am so thankful to God for my wonderful husband who teaches me balance in life. He is certainly my biggest fan, outside of our wonderful son Jawontae'. It was through their love, support, and push that helped me walk into my true identity in freedom.

Forgiveness is an important vehicle towards deliverance. I used to often say, "Forgive yourself!" Christ died that we might live, because He loved us just that much. "If the Son therefore shall make you free, ye shall be free indeed" (Jn. 8:36). Until I truly understood that there is a freedom in God that He can only give and that we don't have the power to forgive ourselves, by picking and choosing what or who to forgive, I remained in bondage. But I found out it is a matter of releasing and no longer holding the person, or situation hostage. Forgiveness is never optional, but always mandatory. Forgiveness doesn't mean we forget, but we just choose to move on and live. I do believe some of our rooted illnesses are caused by harbored unforgiveness. We may have been hurt, but we have also hurt someone as well. There is some hidden pain or struggles that we will probably never share openly, but it doesn't mean we haven't been healed from them. The Word of God states, "A fool vents all his feelings" (Proverbs 29:11). But wisdom will teach us when and what to share openly and the right audience.

When the children of Israel were delivered from Egypt, their greatest challenge was coming out of their mentality of bondage. Mental illness, depression and oppression are real places. Once learning first how to identify, confront & conquer the battle in your mind, it will enable you to move forward in the hope and ability of not looking back. Obstacles will attempt to make us doubt and soul ties and familiarity wants us to continue to look back, but keep moving forward. Deliverance is for everyone and the greatest aspect is hope and wholeness. In the words of the Late Delores Spain, "You can forgive and be free!"

Your Thoughts

Your Thoughts

Your Thoughts

Your Thoughts

Your Thoughts

Chapter 7

Restoration: renewal, original, the act of returning something that was stolen or taken

What has been stolen from you? For me it was my identity, as I walked through the process of penning *Identity Crisis, the Root of Its Beginning*. It was a painful, yet rewarding journey. Never in a million years would I have believed that my life would be where it is at this very moment. As you read in the beginning of this book, I was the least likely to succeed in my family. My sisters were extremely smart and I truly admired them. But I was lost in the attempt to find myself, while harboring unforgiveness towards my biological dad for not being in my life during the early stages until one day, I had to ask myself the following questions. "How long are you willing to remain a hostage to your past? How long are you willing to be the victim, and how long are you willing to wrestle with your identity? As bad as it hurts, how long are you going to make excuses to not excel and just remain stagnated in life?" And then, the process of restoration began.

While growing up, Michael Jackson was my favorite pop singer and my all-time favorite song was "Man in the Mirror"; however, that's one of the hardest things for us to do. Yet,, restoration requires that in order for something to return to it is original state, it must first know what the original looks like. As we grow older in number, so does our appearance and body shape. Maturity is so important because it is a sign of growth. But, a detox has to take place in order for maturity and growth to work hand and hand. Needless to say, I had to mature in many areas.

Our identity is found in Christ alone and not others. No matter what deception is thrown our way, even as it was in the beginning with Adam. God gave Adam dominion in the earth; therefore, the power and authority to walk in the fullness of our own dominion must be restored.

God restored my relationship with my biological father and I am so thankful God restored his life. I was the first in my family to attend college and from there, to pursue multiple degrees, not allowing excuses from my past any longer to hinder my growth. My biological father never missed a graduation; small things do matter. God also restored my relationship with my stepfather as for many years; it was a rocky relationship of dislike towards him due to my brokenness. Let me tell how forgiveness and deliverance were so important for me. In 2009, my stepfather became seriously ill, but God had mended our relationship a couple of years prior to his illness. I am so thankful, that I had the pleasure of being one of my stepfather's caregivers before he transitioned in December of 2012, in which was the highest act of kindness I could've ever given to my stepfather.. I will never forget hearing him saying, "Pray for me baby; I am afraid I will never recover." What blessed me in this, is that I gave him so much trouble growing up, but when I gave my life to Christ, he always respected the God in me and I was able to lead my stepfather to Christ. I am so thankful I didn't stay in comfort mode due to my feelings, which is so easy to do. Time is something you will never regain; it would have been a hard pill to swallow if my stepfather would have transition without our relationship being restored.

Every day I am now learning the importance of keeping a pure heart, not a doormat for anyone, but having my heart clean, making sure my motives, attitude, conversation, and even my responses are pure, which is all a part of being restored. I once heard someone say, "It's not what you do to me that makes you a good fighter, but it is what I do to you that makes me a good fighter!" In others words, there are times you don't have to say anything. "A soft answer turns away wrath, but a harsh word stirs up anger" (Proverbs 15:1). My mom often used to say, "The less you say, and the less you'll have to take back." Oh boy, was she right!

Pride is an inwardly directed emotion that carries two common meanings with negative and/or positive connotations. Pride can hinder us from being restored, which causes conceit, superiority or arrogance. And yet, He still gives more grace. "Wherefore he saith, God resisteth the proud, but giveth grace unto the humble" (James 4:6).

Everything that has been stolen due to the root of bitterness, identity crisis or just from the cares of life, can be restored. I am reminded of the lame man that sat at the pool of Bethesda, who was lame for 38 years. He was so content, and comfortable being around what was familiar. It's very easy to do that when we don't have anyone challenging us to be greater; all we see is the pain with excuses of why we can't get better. But just one personal encounter with Jesus can change the course of your life. Jesus asked the lame man one question. "Wilt thou be made whole?" But the lame man offered up an excuse, because he was at a place of hopelessness saying he had no one to help put him in the water. But Jesus told him to rise, take up his bed, and walk! In other words, identify, confront and conquer what has conquered you! And the man followed the words Jesus spoke directly to him. What I love about this story is the lame man didn't have to do what others did by waiting year after year for the water to be trouble. He didn't even have to get in the water, even though he laid there attached to what made him feel comfortable, never even knowing that he could walk and all he had to do was get UP! While walking through this journey called life, I am a firm believer we all need at least one mentor, encourager and critic to help propel us to reach our fullest potential in life. It isn't about who finishes first, or who gains the most. We are not competing with each other, but completing one another. A great leader always adds value. As you read this, it is my prayer no matter how long the infirmities have been there, get up and walk into total restoration, one step at a time. God can heal us everywhere we hurt! "I will restore to you the years that the swarming locust has eaten, the cankerworm, and the caterpillar, and the palmerworm, my great army which I sent among you" (Joel 2:25).

Your Thoughts

Your Thoughts

Your Thoughts

Your Thoughts

Your Thoughts

Chapter 8

Walking In Victory!
Victory: a success or superior position achieved against an opponent, opposition and difficulty

So many go through life struggling from day to day, from hour to hour, from month to month and even year to year, walking in defeat not knowing VICTORY belongs to them. The facts are there will always be someone more educated, intelligent, handsome, prettier, taller, smaller, and better career. But the truth is, that doesn't mean our life isn't significant and doesn't have purpose. No longer will we remain a hostage of our own insecurities or identity crisis, always fishing for validation or praises of others to determine our worth. In the words of Eleanor Roosevelt, "No one can make you feel inferior without your consent." In other words, we hold the key! Never dim your light to make others comfortable. Our purpose is greater than the opinion of others!

I truly believe validation and compliments from others are good at times, but we must not get addicted to them. To walk in victory, we have to know that there is a treasure in us, there is value in us; not just what we carry on the outside, but most importantly what is on the inside of us. In writing this book I didn't realize the many hidden wounds I suppressed for years through my own writings. While revisiting certain issues, healing and liberation has taken place even the more in my life. My prayer is the same for every reader that no matter how deeply rooted the issue or pain may be, I truly believe we are in an hour that physical, emotional, and financial healing are getting ready to take place. "But you are a chosen generation, a royal priesthood, a holy nation, His own special people, that you may proclaim the praises of Him who called you out of darkness into His marvelous light" (I Peter 2:9). The pattern has changed; no longer will we be identified according to our old methods. Our value comes from God alone; we have worth because of what God did, not because of what we did. Royalty, peace, and happiness belongs to us; therefore, we have to stop being afraid to walk in victory due to the fear of the unknown that paralyzes movement. Our movement is crucial in this hour and we must be faith walkers. "Let us hold fast the profession of our faith without wavering; for he is faithful that promised" (Hebrew 10:23).

We can no longer get stuck watching the clock, but do what the clock does and that's move, even though our dreams, desire, and promises haven't come to fruition yet. He is faithful that promised so walk in victory for we are more than conquerors. Speak life instead of defeat. Start making a confession over your life every day. Finally, be strong in the Lord and in his mighty power; we can't and will never be able to do it in our own strength. "But, thanks be to God! He gives us the victory through our Lord Jesus Christ" (1 Cor. 15:57).

Now that we are walking in victory, let's make some personal confessions:

- *We are walking in victory from Identity Crisis!*
- *We are walking in victory from generational curses, known and unknown!*
- *We are walking in victory from mental and emotional bondages, oppression, suppression and possession!*
- *We are walking in victory from anxiety, stress and worry!*
- *We are walking in victory from the opinions of others!*
- *We are walking in victory from unforgiveness, bitterness and resentment!*
- *We are walking in victory from poverty and lack!*

- *We are walking in victory from the spirit of suicide, physical and spiritual bullying!*
- *We are walking in victory from false humility, soul ties, sickness, and disease!*

Now that we have made our personal confessions, no one has the power to undo our words but us! Although life happens, the way to continue to combat darkness is to quickly identify, confront and conquer the stronghold while making our walking in victory confessions. "For the weapons of our warfare are not carnal, but mighty through God to the pulling down of strongholds" (II Cor. 10:4).

We have the VICTORY over every opponent, difficulty, and opposition for we were created in the image of Christ and in His likeness. We were given dominion and the authority in advance before any obstacle, opposition, trial, or hardship occurred. Remember we have power in Christ; the tricks of the enemy never change for he only comes to steal, kill and destroy. When you know who are, the root of your identity crisis can longer rob you. It's about being the best you, and no longer walking in anyone else's shadow. YOU CAN OVERCOME!

Your Thoughts

Your Thoughts

Your Thoughts

Your Thoughts

Your Thoughts

www.ingramcontent.com/pod-product-compliance
Lightning Source LLC
Chambersburg PA
CBHW070546300426
44113CB00011B/1811